Algrove Publishing Limited
36 Mill Street, P.O. Box 1238
Almonte, Ontario, Canada K0A 1A0

Telephone: (613) 256-0350
Fax: (613) 256-0360
Email: sales@algrove.com

National Library of Canada Cataloguing in Publication

Hobbs, Edward W
    Sailing ships at a glance / Edward W. Hobbs ; with an
introduction by L.G. Carr Laughton.

(Classic reprint series)
Reprint. Originally published: London : Architectural Press, 1925.
Includes bibliographical references and index.
ISBN 1-897030-02-9

    1. Sailing ships--History. 2. Sailing ships--History--Pictorial works.
I. Title. II. Series: Classic reprint series (Almonte, Ont.)

VM15.H62 2004   623.82'03'09   C2004-901354-8

Printed in Canada
#1-7-04

PUBLISHER'S NOTE

It takes a brave author to summarize the styles of thousands of years of sailing vessels in just a hundred pages. That he did it well is evidenced by the willingness of the eminent L.G. Carr Laughton to write a foreword. As Carr Laughton notes, Edward Hobbs was well qualified to introduce a novice to this vast subject.

Leonard G. Lee
Publisher
July, 2004
Almonte, Ontario

How We Make Our Books - *You may not have noticed, but this book is quite different from other softcover books you might own. The vast majority of paperbacks, whether mass-market or the more expensive trade paperbacks, have the pages sheared and notched at the spine so that they may be glued together. The paper itself is often of newsprint quality. Over time, the paper will brown and the spine will crack if flexed. Eventually the pages fall out.*

All of our softcover books, like our hardcover books, have sewn bindings. The pages are sewn in signatures of sixteen or thirty-two pages and these signatures are then sewn to each other. They are also glued at the back but the glue is used primarily to hold the cover on, not to hold the pages together.

We also use only acid-free paper in our books. This paper does not yellow over time. A century from now, this book will have paper of its original color and an intact binding, unless it has been exposed to fire, water, or other catastrophe.

There is one more thing you will note about this book as you read it; it opens easily and does not require constant hand pressure to keep it open. In all but the smallest sizes, all our books will also lie open on a table, something that a book bound only with glue will never do unless you have broken its spine.

The cost of these extras is well below their value and while we do not expect a medal for incorporating them, we did want you to notice them.

SAILING SHIPS
AT A GLANCE

A PICTORIAL RECORD OF THE EVOLUTION OF
THE SAILING SHIP FROM THE EARLIEST
TIMES UNTIL TO-DAY

BY
EDWARD W. HOBBS, A.I.N.A.
Vickers Gold Medallist

WITH AN INTRODUCTION BY
L. G. CARR LAUGHTON

LONDON
1925

Algrove Publishing
Classic Reprint Series

INTRODUCTION

THERE are several reasons why men of the English race love old ships. That which lies deepest, and is therefore least often explicitly avowed even to ourselves, is that we know, most of us subconsciously, that our ships were the prime instruments whereby England, in the course of a few centuries, raised herself from the position of a small island kingdom to that of a mighty empire. Regarded in this way a love of ships is a manifestation of the pride of race. We are thus predisposed to love our ships as valued old friends which have earned both gratitude and honour in our service, in trade and in discovery no less than in war. And when we make the acquaintance of the old ships which did the work for us before men thought of putting engines into their holds, we find much to admire in them.

There is an æsthetic appeal in the grace of form which was their outward symbol of efficiency, in the symmetry of their rigging, in the lights and shades of their swelling canvas, and in the profuse ornamentation to which they readily lent themselves. The appeal is heightened by a sense of regret that so much of man's best handiwork

INTRODUCTION

has had its day. There is an appeal of a different nature
in the technical development whereby men of many races
and many ages adapted ships to their varying needs,
thus calling into existence a great diversity of types.
We stand to learn much from the study of these types
and of the manner of their handling. Some knowledge
of them is necessary to such as would read with full
understanding the almost unlimited history of man's
activity by sea. Without it we cannot appreciate the
work of Columbus or of Cook; nor can we put ourselves
in the position of the many daring pioneers of overseas
trade, from the nameless Minoans who made Crete a
trade centre of the Mediterranean, to merchant adven-
turers of the type of Willoughby and Middleton, or to
the hardy navigators of more recent time who, undeterred
by the perils of the sea, took, and still take, their ships
to the ends of the earth if they see therein any prospect
of advantage.

Neither, without this knowledge, can we appreciate
the genius of great sea-commanders. In movements to
intercept or to guard against an enemy, in blockade and
in battle, the ships are the tools of an admiral's trade.
To know how our Navy has many times saved England
from invasion, to understand how sea-battles were fought,
or how the vital trade of the country has been protected
through long wars, it is necessary to know at least something of what ships could and could not do. It is hard
indeed to say where the usefulness of a study of ships

INTRODUCTION

ends: ethnologists, for instance, find in the ships of primitive peoples valuable evidence from which to deduce the history of migrations and of the interrelationship of early races.

The advent of steam certainly robbed the seas of some of their charm. It is an exaggeration to say that there is no beauty in the ships of this generation: beauty there is, less than in the days of sail, and of a widely different kind; but it is a beauty which depends more than ever on its expression of efficiency, so that its appeal is directed primarily to those who know in what efficiency consists. There is majesty in great men-of-war, stateliness in liners, and a purposeful trimness about the better classes of cargo steamers; but on the other hand it must be confessed that some shipowners, or shipbuilders, seem to scorn appearances, and to make what may almost be called a direct cult of frank ugliness, as though seemliness were antagonistic to efficiency.

This phase, it is to be hoped, will pass; especially as the ugliness of which a steamer is capable is greatly more obtrusive than that of the clumsiest of the sea-waggons of the sailing era. The ugliness of the hull of a sailing ship might be in great measure redeemed by her spars and sails, to which even stains and patches gave a certain picturesqueness, such as is foreign to rusty plates, misplaced stump masts, and bristling derricks and samson-posts. The masts and sails had at least to be proportioned to the ship, or they would not drive and work her, and this proportion was evident and pleasing to the eye. The most utilitarian steamer, too, must observe certain rules of order and proportion; but she can, and not seldom does, conceal her observance of them in her engine-room, and, as it were in protest against her concession to law and order, covers herself with ungainly excrescences above deck.

And yet, sheer and unnecessary ugliness notwithstanding, there remains some degree of interest in every craft that floats. She exists to brave the sea, and by that fact alone, if by no other, commends herself to our respect. It is good to see ships in harbour, to appraise their proportions, and speculate on how they would behave in such and such conditions. It is better to meet them in a sea-way, and to observe how correlated form and power, man's handiwork, meet and overcome the forces of nature. But best of all is to have control of the vessel, however small, which at the call of the sea wakes, as it seems, into a sentient being. To the many who have these tastes, and know the spell of the sea, ships are endowed with a personality of their own. They live; they pass from life; but even so they live on in something more than a memory. It is their enduring courage that stands out above their other qualities; for any ship that is seaworthy and seakindly has the power of endearing herself and commanding respect. Ships have sailed a long way, and men with them, since Horace wrote his " Illi robur et æs triplex," when his thoughts turned to the

INTRODUCTION

first man who braved the sea; but we still treat the god
of the sea with careful respect, knowing that his strength
is virtually without limit. It does not do to forget that
whoever entrusts his life or goods to the sea, even in the
mightiest of ships, gives hostages to fortune. You may
hear fishermen refer familiarly but deferentially to that
god known to seamen as Davy Jones from time out of
mind. As a half apology for some fitting that may look
unnecessarily strong, one will say: "He's very strong, is
Davy"; and another's condemnation of scamped work
or neglect may take the form of "He won't have it,
won't Davy."

But if the interest of the study of ship-lore is great,
its vastness and complexity are commensurate. Probably
no one has ever made a calculation of the number of
different ship-types which have existed since the dawn
of history, nor indeed would it be possible to do so. But
it may be calculated roughly that even from the days
of Elizabeth to the present there have been, of English
ships and vessels alone, probably at least 500 major
types, which again might be almost minutely subdivided.
How many, then, have there been among all nations
throughout the ages? And yet some at least of us would
wish to know all that is to be known of all these ships.
It is no deterrent, but an incentive rather to us, that
relatively to what is to be learnt no one knows much.
Enough is known to give us a sound general idea of the
course which development has taken, and we are able

INTRODUCTION

thereby to understand what the owners of those many ships could do with them. If we wish to know more we must seek for ourselves, adding thereby to the common fund of knowledge.

But before we can come to the task of original research we must know what has already been made available. In other words, we must study the published literature of the subject; and in doing so we will not unnaturally begin with the less specialised treatises. To introduce a beginner, who wants to know how to tell a brig from a schooner, or a West Indiaman from a frigate, to the study of ship-lore by giving him to read a learned disquisition on some highly technical and controversial point, such as may be found occasionally in antiquarian publications, would be as wise as to introduce a boy to the integral calculus before he had made the acquaintance of decimal fractions.

There have been published of late many books on the evolution of shipping, some few of them worth commendation. It may be said that even the most inaccurate of them—and many of them are highly inaccurate even within the limits of well-ascertained fact—has at least some merit so long as the author has avoided dulness. He may have succeeded in attracting another to the study of the subject.

It is, I think, one of the chief merits of Mr. Hobbs's book that he displays the attractiveness of the subject,

INTRODUCTION

because he himself is inspired by it. He has contented himself with a minimum of text, employing only enough to explain and connect the many line drawings which form the principal feature of the book. This, as it seems to me, is the manner in which the study of the subject can best be approached. It makes the path smooth for the student: it leads him on imperceptibly towards the heights. But it is a method particularly trying for the author. An artist cannot express doubts and hedge; he is bound by the limits of his craft to be categorical. He cannot say: " This is what I think a Greek trireme of the Peloponnesian War looked like, but the evidence is scanty and conflicting, and I may very well be wrong on such and such points." The writer can say this to his desire, marshalling his evidence with learned care; but the artist has to commit himself. He is limited to saying to his public " This is a trireme." At most he can shift the responsibility a little by inserting a title to say that the drawing is after such an ancient representation, or reconstructed from descriptions or references in such another ancient author. But the responsibility of a definite statement remains with him. And this difficulty pervades the whole subject.

There are those who have taken this responsibility lightly; who have reproduced any older drawing without considering its lack of authority. Such authors find their place, and in a little while are read no more. There are others, not so many in number, who recognise that they

INTRODUCTION

have put their hand to a serious task, and therefore do
their best to qualify themselves for it by care and thought.
They are the men whom it is advisable to choose as
guides. They will not lead us to the heights in one stage.
The student will find that after each stage comes a halt
to prepare him for a steeper ascent, which gradually
becomes a scramble towards a summit approached by
a precipice. If his love of the subject has been awakened
by his first guide he will not be deterred by prospective
difficulties; he will be content to know that the path set
for him provides good sound footing, not slipping screes.
The purpose of this Introduction is to say that in my
opinion Mr. Hobbs has been at pains both to choose a
good path and to show how attractive it is.

L. G. CARR LAUGHTON.

ADMIRALTY, S.W. I.
October, 1925.

PREFACE

THE glamour of the sailing ship is unlikely to be effaced from the memory of insular peoples who in the past have of necessity largely built up their place in the world with the aid of sailing ships. This work is an endeavour to show briefly and in a pictorial manner something of the evolution of the sailing ship from the earliest times until the present day.

The author is fully aware of the magnitude of the task, that it is a subject of great difficulty, and that it is impossible, in this book, to do more than indicate some of the phases through which the sailing ship has passed.

Many of the illustrations are based on tradition or conjecture, but, so far as is practicable, an attempt has been made to reconstruct these fascinating vessels from contemporary evidence and to present them as actual ships in active pursuit of their vocation.

In general, the illustrations are of characteristic ships of the period. They are not submitted as being meticulously detailed, indeed to do so would require many similar volumes. Although every year increases the store of knowledge of old ships, much has yet to be discovered. Probably no other sphere offers such scope for the studious explorer to unearth facts and information

PREFACE

which may entirely alter the present comprehension of the evolution of the sailing ship.

The author desires to express his grateful thanks to all those who have assisted in the preparation of this work, and especially to his friend Mr. L. G. Carr Laughton for invaluable information and courteous and ungrudging help.

The work will not have been in vain if you, reader, use this book simply as a gateway to a great world. Through it, the imaginative mind, guided by fragmentary evidence surviving from times long since passed, may voyage in fancy to the golden west, discover fresh territories, learn of strange peoples, hear unknown tongues, and glimpse something of the endeavour, the heroism, and the agony of the early mariners in their contest with the eternal sea.

EDWARD W. HOBBS.

CATERHAM VALLEY.
October, 1925.

CONTENTS

ILLUSTRATIONS

SPECIALLY PREPARED FOR THIS WORK BY THE AUTHOR

ILLUSTRATIONS

ILLUSTRATIONS

THE EVOLUTION OF THE HULL AND SAIL

Non-technical readers will perhaps be glad of an explanation of some elementary terms which will be used for convenience throughout this book. That part of the ship which is in the water is known as the under-water body, and the part above as the freeboard. The hull, which is the principal part of the vessel, comprises these two portions. There are many differences in ships, and a great many names used when referring to them or their components, but for simplicity the following terms will be used. The key is given in Fig. 1, showing diagrammatically the hull of a ship cut away to reveal part of the interior.

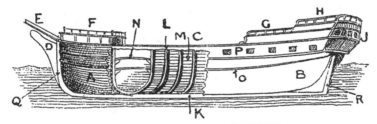

FIG. 1. PARTS OF THE HULL.

Named and described in the text.

A = Bow.	J = Stern.
B = Stern.	K = Keel.
C = Waist.	L = Ribs, or timbers.
D = Headknee, or cut-water.	M = Planking.
	N = Deck beam.
E = Bowsprit.	O = Wales, or bends.
F = Forecastle.	P = Ports.
G = Quarter deck.	Q = Stem.
H = Poop.	R = Stern post.

TECHNICAL TERMS

The rudder is hung on the stern post.

The masts and standing rigging—that is, the cordage

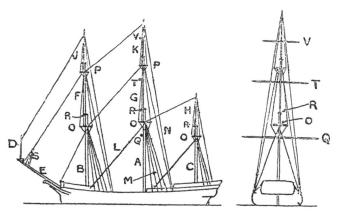

FIG. 2.   MASTS AND SOME RIGGING.

Shown diagrammatically for purposes of identification.

used to support the masts—are shown in Fig. 2, and are named as follows:

A = Main mast.
B = Fore mast.
C = Mizen mast.
D = Spritsail topmast.
E = Bowsprit.
F = Fore topmast.
G = Main topmast.
H = Mizen topmast.
J = Fore topgallant mast.
K = Main topgallant mast.

L = Main stay.
M = Main shrouds.
N = Main back stays.
O = Top.
P = Cross trees.
Q = Main yard.
R = Cap.
S = Crow's-foot attachment.
T = Topsail yard.
V = Topgallant yard.

The yards are used for spreading the sails and all are named according to the mast on which they hoist—*e.g.*, main topsail yard and main topsail, because they are hoisted on the main topmast. Similarly the stays and shrouds are distinguished by the name of the mast which they support—*e.g.*, main stays, mizen shrouds. Numerous developments, variations, and differences are found in different vessels which are mentioned in their appropriate places in subsequent chapters.

THE EVOLUTION OF THE HULL

The evolution of ships has not been a matter of pure chronology, but apparently is more affected by social developments and geographical considerations. The earliest records of ships have been obtained from Egypt, and for thousands of years the hull is of the general character shown diagrammatically in Fig. 3, which is crescent-shaped in side view and pointed at each end in plan. Subsequently, the hull became broader or more rounded in plan, and erections were constructed at the bows and stern, thus giving the general character shown in Fig. 4, although they do not always project beyond the stem and stern.

Differences rapidly evolved between merchant ships and warships. The merchant ship retained the general character of Fig. 4, and is sometimes known as the round ship, while the early war vessels gradually evolved into something after the style of Fig. 5, or a long ship. The erections at the bow and stern are for the fighting men, while the bulwarks or palisade, sometimes in the form of a projecting gallery along the waist of the ship, protected the rowers and provided for free movement of the fighters. The tapering appendage at the bows, known as the ram, provided a most deadly form of assault.

From this evolved the Mediterranean galley, which remained a characteristic southern vessel for a very long time. Northern ships developed along somewhat different lines, but on almost every water was found the long ship and the round ship. The long ship was long, and so called because oars formed her chief motive power, sails being auxiliary. Having freedom of movement she was the most suitable for war, and became the universal type, and so remained for thousands of years. The round ship no doubt co-existed from a very early date. She was the carrier, and if she had oars they were auxiliary for getting in and out of harbour.

With the introduction of gunpowder and the evolution of the cannon, great changes in ship form took place. This ultimately produced the characteristic ship of Fig. 6, notable for blunt-ended bows and stern, the latter becoming flat, or cut off square as it were, after about A.D. 1500. After this date it increased greatly in height and, with a number of castles at bow and stern, the walls of the hull were pierced with ports to permit of gunfire. Note must be made of the changes in naval tactics with the development of different weapons of assault. With the increased use of cannon, the hulls increased in length and height until they culminated in the famous "wooden walls" (Fig. 7), where two or three decks were provided for guns, and the towering sides of the largest ships were pierced with 100 or more ports. Vessels as Fig. 5 represent the culmination of the pre-gunpowder era, and Fig. 7 the culmination of the sailing warship in the age of cannon.

During the long peace of the Victorian era the sailing ship reached its zenith in the form of the clipper shown diagrammatically in Fig. 8.

The remarkable similarity in early hull form suggests that its evolution is best studied by considering its possible and probable methods of construction. Some think the ship evolved from a dug-out canoe by the addition of planks, as shown in Fig. 9, others hold that it is derived from the simple three-plank hull of Fig. 10. Alternative theories are the use of ribs or a wattle framework covered with skins something like a coracle (see Chapter II). Early Egyptian boats may have been of reeds or papyrus, but from an early age were made with planks, and were ribless and keel-less. Boats of the earliest type could, however, be built with unskilled labour by the method

4

FIG. 3.
AN EARLY FORM OF HULL.
Exhibiting a crescent form and
overhanging ends.

FIG. 4.
A LATER STAGE IN HULL DE-
VELOPMENT.
Exhibiting bow and stern platforms.

FIG. 5. CULMINATION OF THE PRE-
GUN SHIP.

The ram, used for offensive purposes, is a
feature of the bows.

FIG. 6. MEDIÆVAL SHIP
WITH GUNS.

The bowsprit and towering erections
at bow and stern are notable features.

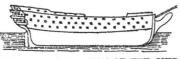

FIG. 7. CULMINATION OF THE SHIP
WITH GUNS.

Towering sides pierced for many guns.

FIG. 8. THE CLIPPER SHIP.

Notable for elegance and speed, and
characterised by fine lines.

FIGS. 3–8. STAGES IN THE EVOLUTION OF HULL FORM.

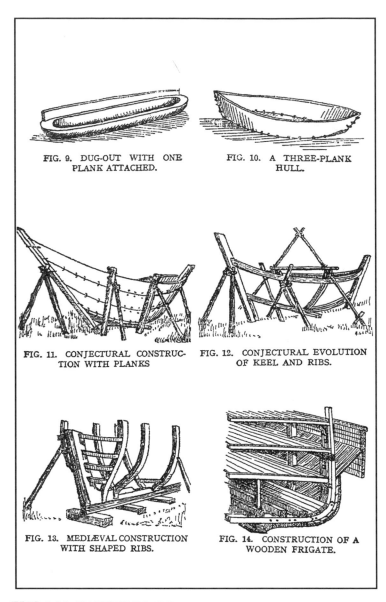

FIG. 9. DUG-OUT WITH ONE PLANK ATTACHED.

FIG. 10. A THREE-PLANK HULL.

FIG. 11. CONJECTURAL CONSTRUCTION WITH PLANKS

FIG. 12. CONJECTURAL EVOLUTION OF KEEL AND RIBS.

FIG. 13. MEDIÆVAL CONSTRUCTION WITH SHAPED RIBS.

FIG. 14. CONSTRUCTION OF A WOODEN FRIGATE.

FIGS. 9–14. VARIOUS FORMS OF EARLY HULL CONSTRUCTION.

pictured in Fig. 11, as ordinary planks will bend naturally until they form such a shape.

The author suggests as a purely conjectural hypothesis that stem and stern posts were set up in the ground, other stakes erected at suitable places, and all supported by struts. The planks which formed the sides and bottom were forced into position against them and lashed with thongs, or otherwise fastened together, and similarly to the stem and stern posts. The lower parts of the stem and stern posts were then cut away, the outer struts removed, and the vessel launched. This would account for the universal decoration and even deification of the stem and stern posts in the early days, as they represent the parents or good qualities of the hull.

The possible evolution of the separate keel and internal ribs from the foregoing is pictured in Fig. 12, the similar elementary arrangement being shown. The keel, either cambered or straight, would be jointed to the stem and stern posts, the internal ribs set up and longitudinal members forming the upper part of the hull then fixed to the ribs, stem, and stern. This system could develop into the mediæval method of construction diagrammatically shown in Fig. 13, where naturally crooked timber is fashioned to form ribs which are jointed to a keel composed of several portions. The rounded stern, being abrupt in form, is shaped with horizontally placed members disposed between the stern post and last rib.

A method of construction in use about 1850 is shown in Fig. 14, where the ribs are built of several portions, and the planking is in part doubled. An inner layer of diagonally placed planks from the turn of the bilge has an outer layer of horizontally placed planks. The upper and lower planks are solid and the deck beams braced with strong iron or steel angles.

THE SAIL

THE EVOLUTION OF THE SAIL

The sail was for thousands of years practically rectangular. An early form shown in Fig. 15 was simply a piece of matting suspended from a horizontal pole lashed to the mast. This evolved into the sail shown in Fig. 16, where two light poles were lashed together to form a yard and supported a sail composed of flax or some similar material. At an early date ropes, known as lifts, were provided on southern ships to support the ends of the yards, and on northern ships at about A.D. 1250. A rope or halyard to move the yard bodily up and down the mast was an early introduction. Braces from the yard arms to the deck and sheets from the bottom corners, or clews of the sail provided the means for controlling it.

To meet varying strengths of wind, an early device is pictured in Fig. 17, known as a bonnet, which was simply an additional sail laced to the bottom of the main sail, which could be removed as requisite. For centuries the square sail was made so that it could be furled with the yard aloft, or alternatively the yard was lowered.

In Roman times the method of furling or shortening sail shown in Fig. 18 was in use, where ropes were run through rings, or the like, sewn on the fore side of the sail so that it could be gathered up either wholly or in part. In the Middle Ages the sails were so cut that they ballooned or bulged like a bag full of wind. A characteristic form is shown in Fig. 19, where the sail forms four definite sections, the centre restrained by a rope called a bowge.

Additional ropes were introduced at an early date, and are shown in Fig. 19. These are: the bowline from the side or leech of the sail to some position near the bows, the martnet or leech lines for gathering up the upper part of the sail, and the bowge to restrain the middle portion of the sail. The tack forwards from the clew of the sail to help in setting it, and the buntline from the foot of the sail, used when reefing or taking it in. Braces, lifts, and

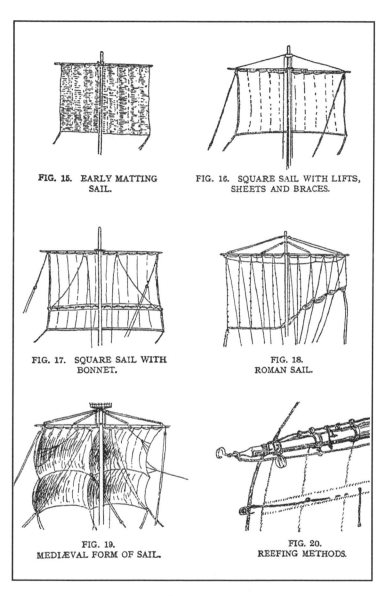

FIG. 15. EARLY MATTING SAIL.

FIG. 16. SQUARE SAIL WITH LIFTS, SHEETS AND BRACES.

FIG. 17. SQUARE SAIL WITH BONNET.

FIG. 18. ROMAN SAIL.

FIG. 19. MEDIÆVAL FORM OF SAIL.

FIG. 20. REEFING METHODS.

FIGS. 15–20. EXAMPLES OF DIFFERENT METHODS OF EMPLOYING SQUARE SAILS.

the like, instead of being single, now became doubled or trebled, using blocks to form a tackle. In later vessels the sail was attached to a rope fixed at the top of the yard, known as a jack stay, shown in Fig. 20, and efforts were made so that the sail when set was as flat as possible.

Reefing methods were by means of reef points, shown at the right corner of Fig. 20, being simply short cords attached to the sail. In later times and about 1854 in the Royal Navy, the reef line shown at the left side of Fig. 20, and the becket, were used, the latter attached

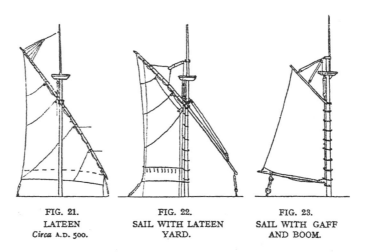

FIG. 21.
LATEEN
Circa A.D. 500.

FIG. 22.
SAIL WITH LATEEN
YARD.

FIG. 23.
SAIL WITH GAFF
AND BOOM.

to the jack stay. In both cases the sail was slackened, the men went up on to the yard, resting their feet on the foot ropes, which had been used by the Romans and then forgotten for 1,000 years or more, and the sail gathered up and reefed.

It should be appreciated that this evolution was not chronological, nor may all the features in the previous illustrations be found on each and every square sail of a given period, the ships of some nations being somewhat different from others. In the southern hemisphere and in

THE GAFF

the Mediterranean the square sail evolved into a triangular sail, called a " lateen," which, adopted in the northern hemisphere, was known as the mizen, and is shown diagrammatically in Fig. 21. It has remained as a lateen in the East until the present day, but western countries evolved from it the spanker or driver, also called the mainsail. First the forward part of the sail was omitted, while the lateen yard was retained, as in Fig. 22. Subsequently, the yard gave place to the gaff (Fig. 23), terminating in a fork, fitting either around the mast, or an additional and vertical parallel spar, and the foot of the sail was spread by a boom.

II

PRIMITIVE CRAFT

Primitive sailing craft of the types illustrated, and many others somewhat similar in character, have no doubt been in use substantially in their present form for countless ages. Evolved by the natural use of material easily accessible to the natives, the construction was necessarily limited by their dexterity and skill. Such craft differ considerably from modern shipwright's work, but are remarkable when the constructional limitations are considered. Crude and elementary as they are, these primitive craft have survived the passage of time, and continue to render admirable service in their own localities and for the purposes of their native owners.

The balsa, or raft (Fig. 24), is one of the earliest forms of sailing ship, and consists of a number of logs lashed together with cross members. The little erection amidships is for merchandise or passengers, and sometimes had a raised floor to keep the merchandise dry.

Another primitive native craft is the catamaran (Fig. 25). This consists of a central hull, often a dugout or some primitive construction, with two or more poles lashed across the hull projecting on either side, where they are fastened to substantial logs. An elementary form of sail and a steering paddle complete the craft.

A peculiar craft woven from reeds is shown in Fig. 26, and hails from Bolivia. These craft are used on Lake Titicaca, a great inland lake some 12,000 feet above sea-level. The boats are made in this way as no wood is available locally. They are quite shapely, and appear to answer their purpose admirably.

FIG. 24.   A BALSA OR RAFT.

Primitive form of native sailing boat.

FIG. 25.   A NATIVE CATAMARAN.

A boat midway between a raft and a sailing canoe.

13

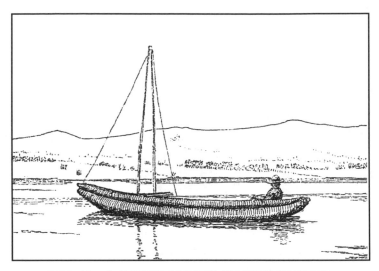

FIG. 26.   A BOLIVIAN BOAT OF WOVEN REED.

Shapely and efficient despite the nature of the material.

FIG. 27.   A THIBETAN OR MONGOLIAN VESSEL.

Showing the use of vertical side planks.

THE CORACLE

The fourth example, shown in Fig. 27, is a Thibetan or Mongolian vessel of unknown antiquity, reconstructed from a temple wall painting of A.D. 1525. The boat has vertical planks, a simple form of cabin apparently with a raised floor, while the sail is interesting, as it is tied directly to a vertical pole or mast. It simply forms a wind-bag.

FIG. 28. EARLY CORACLE, ONE OF THE PARENTS OF THE MAJESTIC SAILING SHIP.

The coracle (Fig. 28), although not a sailing ship, is here mentioned, as it may have been one of the parents of the majestic ships of to-day and yesterday. It was one of the earliest forms of composite construction, with ribs, a wickerwork body, and a skin covering.

III

SHIPS DURING THE DAWN OF HISTORY

Evidence of the earliest known ships is found in connection with the Egyptian and other peoples along the banks of the Nile. The evidence, mostly pieced together from representations found on vases, wall paintings, models, and so forth, indicates that ships from undated times were definitely advanced in development, as even the earliest exhibits considerable constructive ability.

Amongst the latest discoveries is a small model of a boat pictured in Fig. 29, which dates probably to 10000 B.C. It certainly belongs to a time earlier than the so-called prehistoric, and is known to Egyptologists as Badarian. The model was found in the Fayoum, and may have been propelled by a sail, but of this evidence is still lacking. The model, however, shows a thoroughly ship-shape form, with a counter-stern, probably occupied by the steersman and chief personages, or may have been used for fishing. The hull form, suggesting a square sail may have been used, somewhat as sketched.

Unfortunately, the representations on vases and on some of the wall paintings are such that they leave a great deal to the imagination. The early ship representations on vases are, by competent authorities, set at a period of approximately 6000 B.C. A conjectural representation of such a craft is pictured in Fig. 30. Apparently the hull was built up in some way, probably with a series of rough planks, the mast being made from

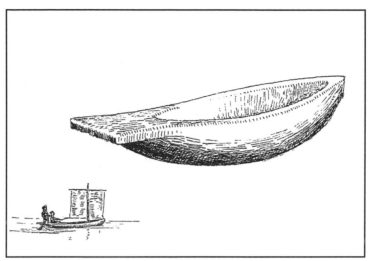

FIG. 29.   A BADARIAN SHIP MODEL.

Circa 10000 B.C.

Probably the oldest in existence.

FIG. 30.   A CONJECTURAL RECONSTRUCTION OF AN EARLY
EGYPTIAN CRAFT.

Circa 6000 B.C.

A palm-tree trunk used as a mast.

17

the trunk of a palm tree. It would appear also that this mast was fastened to the hull by the primitive but fairly obvious method of using the tree roots as natural angles or knees and lashing them to the fabric of the hull.

The existence of an extremely high stern post suggests that another tree-trunk or tall pole was used at the stern to support the mast and yard from which the sail, composed of a kind of matting, was suspended. The sail was very crude, and the vessel obviously could only be used for sailing before the wind. Rowers were employed for manœuvring and for travelling when the wind was not propitious. The owner or captain stood under an awning in the waist of the ship, a rough platform provided shade and accommodation for passengers, and the roof formed a natural storage place for vessels of water, grain, or other products. Steering was effected by a large paddle.

About 1,500 years later, Egyptian ships are represented as provided with a tripod mast with a number of back stays. A vessel of this type is pictured in Fig. 31, and may represent the appearance of a vessel of about the period 4700 B.C.

The hull now exhibits a certain development. It would appear to be definitely stronger and the whole far more seaman-like in appearance and performance. Three steersmen with paddles are located at the stern, and stand under an awning. The usual crew of rowers is provided, the sail, loftier and larger than on earlier ships, is spread by a yard attached to the top of the mast and controlled by a man seated at an eminence at the stern of the ship. The sheets are under the control of a man located in the waist of the ship. The owner, armed with the customary whip or courbash, stands under the awning amidships.

According to Professor W. M. Flinders Petrie, wood was extensively used for Egyptian shipbuilding about the close of the Third Dynasty, probably an imported fir,

FIG. 31. AN EGYPTIAN SHIP.

Circa 4700 B.C.

The tripod mast and back stays are features of interest.

19

spruce, or cedar. Senoferu, about 4700 B.C., is stated to have built sixty ships in one year, and in the same year imported forty ships built of cedar, and it would be interesting to know whence they came. The art of the woodworker at this early age was very well developed, and all wooden structures show great operative skill. The ships would therefore be expected to exhibit a like craftsmanship, and could well have been fine specimens of the shipwright's art.

Vessels of about the period usually assigned to the Ark—that is, about 2800 B.C.—also show a further hull development. The hull is longer in proportion to its beam, and probably fashioned from prepared planks fastened together with pegs. It would be interesting to know whether a keel and ribs were employed at this period, but there is some reason for supposing that this was not the case. The tripod mast is still retained, but in some examples is mounted on a kind of tabernacle, consisting of upright pieces firmly built on to the hull structure and provided with a pivot which supports two of the legs of the tripod. In some early models the tripod is shown counter-weighted by heavy stones to facilitate erection. Fore and back stays appear, and the sail was apparently hoisted by means of lifts and halyards. The sail was controlled by braces and sheets, and was probably made of linen or some similar material.

Although these Egyptian vessels were so highly developed there is at present no evidence of the existence of similar advancement in Western and Northern Europe, where the boats in all probability were nothing more than dug-out canoes or coracles.

IV

EARLY SHIPS

Egyptian boats of about the period 1600 B.C. were in a marked stage of development. The illustration (Fig. 32) shows a vessel employed in the Punt Expedition under Queen Hatshepu. This memorable and famous expedition, which returned safely to Egypt, was probably a voyage to the present Somaliland judging from the nature of the booty which was brought back.

Vessels of this period were used in the Red Sea trade, and exhibit a peculiarity in shipbuilding in the use of the truss. It consisted of a very strong rope or ropes fastened low down to the stem and stern, and to ropes which encircled the hull. It was stretched tightly over uprights attached to cross members at the bottom of the hull, and also fastened to the mast. The purpose of the truss was to stiffen the hull and prevent it from hogging, and suggests that the hull was constructed of separate planks, but without a keel, ribs, or wales. The truss overcame this difficulty to some extent by converting the structure into a kind of trussed beam.

The sail was far larger and probably made of flax or some woven material somewhat analogous to the modern sail cloth. It had a two-piece yard and a boom. The accommodation was better and provided ample storage space for goods and provisions, with accommodation for various important functionaries engaged in the expedition. Steering was effected by a paddle controlled by a tiller, giving the steersman considerable mechanical advantage. The arrangements of the ropes on the yard

FIG. 32. AN EGYPTIAN SHIP.

Circa 1600 B.C.

The heavy rope truss was used to strengthen the hull.

and on the boom are interesting, and their use apparently was for furling the sail. The disposition of the stays and braces and the arrangement of the structure at the masthead suggests an advanced knowledge.

Apparently rollers were used instead of blocks for guiding the ropes.

A battleship of the time of Rameses III, about 1200 B.C., is illustrated in Fig. 33. The palisade along the sides of the vessel protected the rowers from attack, and is a notable feature, as also are the erections at the bow and stern for protection of the fighting men.

The Phœnicians are known to have been great seafaring people, and to have had a marked influence on the development of sea-power, but knowledge of the form of their vessels is meagre. The illustration (Fig. 34) is based on a vessel drawn on a gold gemel ring found in Malta, and undoubtedly of Phœnician origin. The vessel has six rowers a side, carries a small square sail forward and a simple shelter at the stern. Steering is by means of a side paddle. The ram-like projection at the bows was probably used as a ram for offensive purposes, but on trading expeditions enabled the vessel to be put ashore on a sandy beach and then provided a natural gangway.

The development of shipping in the Mediterranean evolved a type of craft notable for its multiplicity of rowers. There is much speculation and argument as to the disposition of the rowers and the form of the ships; but most of it is conjectural. One class of vessel in the form of an open galley with a ram, sheltered forecastle, twenty-five rowers a side, and two small square sails, is illustrated in Fig. 35, and may represent a Greek penteconter about 500 B.C.

A bireme hoisting two larger square sails and propelled by a double bank of rowers is shown in Fig. 36. The gangway or projection at the side of the ship for the fighting men is a notable feature.

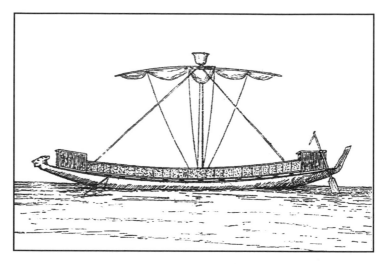

FIG. 33. AN EGYPTIAN BATTLESHIP.

Circa 1200 B.C.

Showing a topcastle on the mast.

FIG. 34. A PHŒNICIAN SHIP.

Circa 750 B.C.

Phœnician ships were amongst the most efficient in their own day.

FIG. 35. A CONJECTURAL RECONSTRUCTION OF A GREEK
PENTECONTER.

Date 500 B.C.

An early form of two-masted ship.

FIG. 36. A CONJECTURAL RECONSTRUCTION OF A GREEK
BIREME.

Circa 300 B.C.

The double banks of oars are a feature of such boats.

FIG. 37. A GREEK UNIREME.

Circa 250 B.C.

Under full sail on a favouring wind.

THE OCULUS

A Greek unireme under sail is shown in Fig. 37. Here the features are the ram, the projecting bulwarks, and the large square sail. Steering was effected, as was customary, with a side paddle. These ships relied on their oars for propulsion, the sails only being used in favourable winds. The Oculus, or eyes painted on the bows of ships at about this time, was probably based on the theory that the boat was a kind of fish and needed eyes to see where it was going. The practice is maintained until the present day on some Far Eastern native vessels.

V

THE ROMAN AND EARLY CHRISTIAN ERA

Roman ships marked several improvements on the earlier Mediterranean vessels, partly due to the natural evolution of the sailing ship, but to some extent arising from the customs and mode of thought of the Romans, who built for durability. Their constructional work is characterised by robustness and solidity. The favourite materials were fir and oak, and existing examples exhibit excellent craftsmanship. The Romans built the hull with separate planks fastened to ribs and sometimes with two or three layers of skins. The joints were made with draw tongues—that is, comparatively thin slips of wood fitted into recesses or mortices fashioned in the joint faces of the planking and secured with pegs.

There were several classes of Roman ships. The fighting ships (Fig. 38) or war vessels appear to have had a projecting platform at about deck level, and at the bows a raised platform protected by a bulwark, and also projecting over the ship's side. At the stern was another platform for the steersman and others. This platform, or poop, was generally covered with an awning or a more permanent structure, and probably formed the living accommodation for the principal officers on board.

Anchors and a ship's boat formed part of the normal equipment, and the whole ship appears to be well furnished. A single square sail was generally used for propulsion, although in the merchantmen an additional square sail was used on a forwardly projecting fore mast something

28

FIG. 38. A ROMAN WARSHIP.

Circa 200 B.C.

Note the wicked-looking but efficient ram on the bows.

29

FIG. 39. A ROMAN MERCHANTMAN.

Circa 100 B.C

The sail plan is characteristic and effective.

30

FIG. 40.   A CONJECTURAL RECONSTRUCTION OF THE WRECK
OF ST. PAUL.   *Circa* A.D. 50.

The story of the voyage and wreck of St. Paul is one of the world's masterpieces of descriptive
writing.

FIG. 41. A LIBURNIAN GALLEY.

Circa A.D. 100.

Fast light galleys used for scouting.

FIG. 42. AN EARLY MERCHANTMAN.

Circa A.D . 100.

Familiar along the coasts of the Mediterranean and Southern Europe.

like a bowsprit, and occasionally a triangular, or "raffee," topsail hoisted above the main sail.

The Roman merchant ship was of somewhat different type, and relied chiefly on sails for propulsion. In many cases a second and smaller sail was mounted on a fore mast somewhat as in Fig. 39. This mast, or a separate spar, appears to have been used as a derrick for hoisting merchandise from the quay or elsewhere. It may have been in a ship of this class that St. Paul made his voyages. The Biblical story adds several points of enlightenment to the store of knowledge of ships of the period, particularly mentioning sailors with the requisite knowledge to manœuvre the ship, and also the use of a small boat for laying out the anchor, and to some extent indicates a three-masted ship which may well have been along the lines shown in Fig. 40.

The marvellous organisation of the Roman Empire made international travel a practical possibility, and must have had a stabilising and consolidating effect on ship design. To some extent the dawn of the Christian era marks the close of the primary phase of ship evolution—the use of large vessels propelled by oars and only propelled by sails when winds were favourable.

These ships, both in Roman and earlier times, had no doubt attained a great size. A vessel sunk in Lake Nemi appears to have been over 200 feet in length, while one found in London would have been some 90 feet or so in length. Thus far, the world had evolved a great ship propelled by many rowers—warships with a ram, fast, light galleys such as the Liburnian shown in Fig. 41, and several classes of very broad merchantmen, examples such as those of Figs. 39 and 42, the former for long voyages, and the latter for coastal work.

Unfortunately, the development of ships in the Far East has so far remained shrouded in mystery, but they were probably designed more or less on the lines of medieval junks and craft of that character.

VI

THE VIKINGS

The Norsemen were great seafarers, and appear to have effected a definite development in shipbuilding with a suddenness and completeness that was unprecedented. Possibly the Norsemen evolved their craft from the Veneti, but the Viking ships represent a class of vessel hitherto unknown, and it is clear they understood the art of fashioning the under-water body to obtain the minimum resistance to its passage through the water, an art that was lost until about the 19th century.

The lines of the hulls of several contemporary Norse ships dating about the period A.D. 800 have been analysed, and when portrayed as a regulation naval architect's plan, indisputably demonstrate that the lines of these ships were of remarkable quality. It is indeed doubtful if the most able designer of the present day could produce a better vessel to fulfil the contemporary conditions. The craftsmanship was of a very high order. The hull was clinker-built, with a keel and ribs, and planked on the outside in a manner that is, generally speaking, in service to this day.

Several examples of ships of this period are illustrated, and it will be noted that the hull possesses remarkable similarity to the modern ship's boat, of course on a much larger scale. The usual arrangement was to hang the shields of the fighting men along the gunwale as a protection. Steering was effected by a single paddle on the starboard side at the stern, the paddle being supported by a wooden block and leather thongs, and controlled by a tiller.

FIG. 43. A NORSE SHIP AT ANCHOR AT NIGHT.

Circa A.D. 700.

With mast lowered, awnings spread, and watchers on the alert for friend or foe.

FIG. 44. AN EARLY NORSE MERCHANTMAN.

Circa A.D. 800.

Finely modelled and superbly made, these craft were excellent for coastal services.

35

FIG. 45.   A NORSE LONG SHIP OR SNEKKJA.

Circa A.D. 800.

Romantic legend and glowing sagas recount the exploits of these northern ships and
their crews.

36

FIG. 46.   AN ENGLISH SHIP OF THE TIME OF KING ALFRED.
Circa A.D. 900.

Representing the ships from which was ultimately developed the organisation known as the
Royal Navy.

FIG. 47. A CONJECTURAL SHIP OF ANGLO-SAXON DAYS.

Circa A.D. 900.

Having a ram at the bows and the contemporary round stern.

FIG. 48. THE *MORA*. (WILLIAM THE CONQUEROR'S SHIP.)

Circa A.D. 1066.

The lantern at the masthead is a notable detail.

EARLY ENGLISH NAVY

The sail could be hoisted speedily by means of halyards, the yard was provided with braces having blocks and tackle, and the stays were set up with a form of dead eye such as is used in substantially the same way at the present day. Vertical posts along the centre line of the ship supported horizontal poles, often beautifully ornamented with carved heads or the like. An awning could be stretched over these poles and fastened to the ship's sides, and in this way excellent accommodation was provided for the crew, as can be seen in Fig. 43.

The Norse ships were of several classes: the dragons, or warships, about 140 feet long; the snekkjas, or long serpent, with from forty to sixty rowers (Fig. 45); the long ships, chiefly propelled by oars; and small coasting merchantmen, such as Fig. 44.

Probably the most notable first English achievements in shipbuilding were at about the time of King Alfred the Great, roughly A.D. 890. The craft were probably open boats propelled by oar and sail somewhat as Fig. 46. Some evidence suggests the Anglo-Saxons had vessels forming a link between the Mediterranean warship with its ram and the round ship of commerce, such as might be pictured by Fig. 47.

Ships at the time of the Norman invasion (Fig. 48) do not appear to be anything in advance of the earlier Norse ships, and in some respects may have been inferior. They were rather fuller at the bows and stern, and were generally embellished with massive stem and stern posts elaborately carved and decorated. Apparently, two definite ship-types were chiefly employed, first the superior ships forming the units of the Navy, and inferior ships built up on the sea-shore and intended simply for the transport of troops across the Channel. One notable feature on William's ship, the *Mora*, is the large lantern at the masthead to act as a guiding light for a fleet.

VII

THE CRUSADES

The Crusades brought numberless peoples of differing tongues into common cause against the Infidel, and ships of many nationalities were used in collaboration. The use of armour of improved pattern, and changes in the mode of warfare, had their effect on shipping, and many pilgrims had to be carried on shipboard. The great passenger traffic was readily dealt with in simple craft of the round ship or merchantman class.

There is little available evidence of the vessels during the period A.D. 1100-1300, but the conjectural reproductions here given may well indicate their general appearance, and a ship of the time of the Crusades is shown in Fig. 49. The King's ship, *circa* 1250 (Fig. 50), shows traces of Norse thought, but every evidence of the lack of their constructive ability. The structures at bow and stern were generally temporary, but gradually evolved into permanent constructions.

The box-like structure on the mast, known as a top-castle, accommodated a look-out and also fighting men (Figs. 51 and 52). A single sail was in general use, as in the illustration (Fig. 53), *circa* 1340. Larger and later craft, such as the French ships used in Bourbon's expedition against Tunis and Barbary pirates (Fig. 55), had three masts with a square sail on each. A grappling iron was carried on a short bowsprit, which later was equipped with a "comb"—a corrugated shaped device used to guide or secure the bowlines. This is seen in the merchantman (Fig. 56), as well as the cresset at the stern and the supports or bails for an awning.

FIG. 49.   A CRUSADER'S SHIP.

Circa 1200.

Carrying the flower of English chivalry on an expedition against Sal-ah-din.

41

FIG. 50.   A KING'S SHIP.

Circa 1250.

Featuring temporary erections at bow and stern for the use of fighting men.

FIG. 51.   A TOPCASTLE.

Circa 1340.

FIG. 52.   A TOPCASTLE.

Circa 1500.

The latter showing the crane for hoisting the bags of stones for use as missiles.

FIG. 53.   AN ENGLISH SHIP SHOWING A STERN RUDDER.

Circa 1340.

The elevated deck erections are more or less permanent.

FIG. 54.   A SARACEN VESSEL OF ABOUT THE TIME OF THE CRUSADES.

Circa 1350.

Several large ships opposed the Red Cross knights.

FIG. 55. A THREE-MASTED SHIP.

Circa 1390.

Sailing on a punitive expedition against the Barbary pirates.

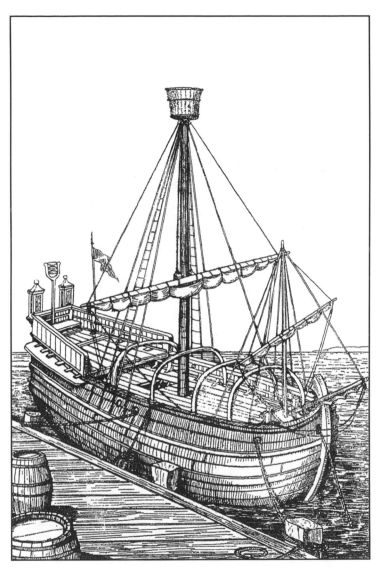

FIG. 56.   A MERCHANTMAN OF THE PERIOD 1390.

Constructive details are here clearly shown.

FIG. 57. A DROMON.

A large galley propelled by oars and sail. *Circa* 1360.

FIG. 58. AN EARLY PERSIAN VESSEL.

Circa 1400.

Unsupported masts and matting sails devoid of braces are used for propulsion.

46

FIG. 59. YARD-ROPE AND
PARREL.

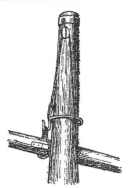

FIG. 60. TRAVELLER AND
UPHAUL.

FIG. 61. CHAIN SLINGS.

FIG. 62. IRON GOOSENECK.

FIG. 63. EARLY THONG LASHING.

FIG. 64. PARREL OF 1450.

EARLY GALLEYS

In the Mediterranean the galley ship persisted, and a dromon is shown in Fig. 57, and a Saracen ship in Fig. 54, both largely conjectural. The rudder hung on the stern post on the centre line of the ship appeared about A.D. 1200 or earlier, and speedily superseded the side paddle for steering purposes.

An early Persian ship is shown in Fig. 58, and has points of similarity with the junks of later days. Figs. 59-64 show details of various methods of supporting the yards on the mast, introduced at widely different periods.

VIII

THE AGE OF ROMANCE

Sailing ships of the period A.D. 1400-1500 are surrounded by romantic legend. As a class they mark a stage in the evolution of seafaring nations, and may perhaps best be considered as inadequate vessels used for stupendous projects. Roughly speaking, seafaring nations at this time seem to have stirred in their sleep and conceived the idea that beyond the apparently limitless oceans there were fertile and rich countries awaiting exploration.

One point worth remembering is that the bulk of the people thought the world was flat, and that the adventurous mariner was quite likely to sail to the literal edge of the ocean and fall off into an eternity of space. Small wonder, then, that Columbus and other great explorers had rather a difficult task in collecting their crews.

A type of three-masted vessel mounting cannon, and dating about 1440, is shown in Fig. 65. Here is shown the rudder hung on the stern post, permanent structures at bow and stern, topcastles on all three masts, each of which carries a small square sail. About this general period the Mediterranean warships were still of the galley form (Fig. 66), hoisting a huge lateen sail. There were also many purely sailing ships, carracks of large size—especially among the Venetians.

A merchantman about the period 1470 is pictured in Fig. 67, and shows an interesting topsail—in this case a true topsail, as it was sheeted to, and handled from, the top. Vessels of this period exhibit outside wales,

FIG. 65.   AN ENGLISH SHIP OF WAR.

Circa 1440.

Three-masted and well-armed—a formidable opponent in a sea fight.

FIG. 66.   A TURKISH GALLEY.

Circa 1455.

The huge lateen sail and single bank of rowers are typical of Mediterranean craft.

FIG. 67.   A MERCHANTMAN.

Circa 1470.

The growth of sea-borne commerce developed a specialized ship of which the above is a
good example.

51

FIG. 68. A FIFTEENTH-CENTURY CARAVEL.

Circa 1490.

Cannon are mounted on the poop—forerunners of the great three-deckers.

FIG. 69. A CARAVEL OF THE TIME OF COLUMBUS.

Circa 1490.

Constructional details of the hull should be noted.

FIG. 70.   A SHIP OF THE TIME OF COLUMBUS.

Circa 1492.

Westward ! to the birth of a great nation.

53

and also the persistence of vertical timbers to strengthen the hull and protect it from damage when coming to port.

The ships of the period were naturally unsuited to long oversea voyages, as they were mostly employed on coastal service. They were in general small vessels, and were often known as caravels. Two examples of this class of craft are illustrated in Figs. 68 and 69. The first is based on drawings by Hansen Burgmair, and is interesting as it shows a form of paddle protruding from the stern about the centre line of the ship. The towering erections at bow and stern are here shown of a more permanent nature, while on the poop are mounted two cannon. Amidships is a temporary erection of timber and canvas apparently for the accommodation of passengers and troops.

The topcastles are substantial, and the main top armed with two small cannon. Two square sails are provided for propulsion, no provision is made for oars, while the beak at the bows acts as a support for the forestay and the bowline. Fig. 69 shows what might be a more accurate representation of a caravel, and is based on an original attributed to Columbus. Here the midship erection is retained, but is less conspicuous. A structure is located on the poop, while the projection forward is interesting, being an integral part of the hull.

A three-masted vessel of about this period is illustrated in Fig. 70, and is of the general character of the ship used by Christopher Columbus on his famous voyage. The poop is here shown as a permanent structure, while the forecastle, although permanent, is somewhat lightly built. It is a three-masted vessel carrying a main topsail, the mizen being a lateen.

IX

THE ELIZABETHAN AGE

The Elizabethan age in the evolution of the sailing ship was one of considerable interest and importance, and there is a good deal of contemporary information about the ships. Perhaps the most notable feature was the extended and widespread use of cannon, and the reliance upon sails only as a means of propulsion, although there were many galleys and other craft in use embodying oars. Cannon had been used for many years prior to the Elizabethan era, but by this time they were largely relied upon as a primary weapon.

This had a marked effect on ship form, as it became necessary to accommodate the guns, which could only be accomplished practically by piercing holes or ports in the sides of the vessel to allow the muzzles to protrude. At first the guns were located low down in the hull, and but little above the water-line, with the result that they could not be utilised in heavy weather. The shipwrights were faced with the great problem in constructing a hull sufficiently strong to withstand the recoil of the guns and also to accommodate their weight, which was considerable.

There were many different sizes and classes of cannon. They were not standardised, and ranged from small pieces, little larger than a blunderbuss, to heavy weapons weighing several tons (Figs. 71 to 76). The hulls were consequently built of very heavy material, mostly oak, and the widest part of the hull was generally at about the water-line. The breadth of the ships was about one-third their length, and above the water-line the sides of the hull

FIG. 71. EARLY BREECH-LOADER "PETRIERSES A BRAGA."

FIG. 72. A GUN OF THE TIME OF HENRY VIIITH.

FIG. 73. AN ELIZABETHAN SWIVEL GUN.

FIG. 74. AN EARLY HOOPED GUN.

FIG. 75. CARRONADE.

FIG. 76. A 32-POUNDER, 1800.

FIGS. 71–76. EVOLUTION OF CANNON USED ON SAILING SHIPS.

FIG. 77. AN ARGOSY OR CARRACK.

Circa 1540.

The *Argosy*—famous in romantic literature.

FIG. 78. A CARRACK.

Circa 1560.

Lumbering merchantmen that often carried rich cargoes.

57

sloped inwards, thus making the upper decks narrower than those below—exactly opposite to the earlier warships.

The sail plan was considerably increased, and many notable inventions were introduced at about this time, including the capstan for weighing the anchor, chain pumps for disposal of the bilge water, the division of the sail plan into a greater number of comparatively smaller units, and the introduction of the top-gallant mast which could be struck—that is, unshipped from its normal position and lowered to the deck or elsewhere.

Similar conditions throughout Europe produced craft with striking points of resemblance, although the ships of each nation had features of their own, and there are many fascinating details to interest the student, but limitation of space prohibits dealing with them at length.

A vessel which may represent a connecting-link between the Elizabethan ships and those of earlier times is the carrack or argosy, shown in Fig. 77. This shows the earlier form of round ship hull, but with more substantial erections at bow and stern. The poop appears in the form of a platform projecting over the sides of the hull somewhat in the form of channels. The hull is pierced for a few guns at unequal levels, and spars and netting cover the waist of the ship as a defence against boarders. The fore and main masts are rigged with square sails, and have small topsails. The mizen mast to some extent exhibits Roman practice, but, as was customary from soon after 1400, carries a lateen.

A further development of this class of ship is shown in Fig. 78, where the bowsprit is longer, the forecastles higher but similar in characteristics, while at the stern there are several superimposed decks, the principal covered with awnings which would be replaced by netting or some other efficient protection during an engagement.

A Spanish galleon is pictured in Fig. 79. This is a four-master. The fore mast carries three square sails, the

FIG. 79. A SPANISH GALLEON.

Circa 1580.

Under full sail during an engagement.

FIG. 80. WESTWARD HO!

Circa 1587.

Ships of this class were used by Drake and other famous explorers.

FIG. 81.   A VENETIAN GALLEAS.

Circa 1588.

An unsuccessful conglomeration of ship types.

FIG. 82.   GALLEYS OR PINNACES OF THE ARMADA DAYS.

Circa 1588.

Many small ships accompanied the Great Armada

FIG. 83.   ONE OF THE SHIPS OF GOOD QUEEN BESS.

Circa 1590.

England's sure shield against the menace of Spain.

FIG. 84.   AN ELIZABETHAN FOUR-MASTED SHIP.

Circa 1590.

Fierce fights, tender love, and high adventure invest these old ships with a wondrous human appeal.

FIG. 85.
BELOW DECKS, SHOWING
RIDING BITTS.

FIG. 86. THE WHIPSTAFF, SHOWN
IN PART SECTION TO REVEAL
THE METHOD OF CONSTRUCTION
AND WORKING.

FIG. 87.
CAPSTAN ON DECK.

FIG. 88. CAPSTAN BETWEEN DECKS,
ACTUATED FROM ABOVE.

FIGS. 85–88. INTERIOR VIEWS OF ELIZABETHAN SHIPS.

Circa 1580.

main mast is similarly rigged, while the mizen and bona-
venture both use lateen sails. The open gallery or
balcony-like structure at the stern is interesting, as are
the overhanging stern cabins.

A vessel of the type that made long overseas voyages
is pictured in Fig. 80, and is of the general type used by
Drake, Frobisher, and other celebrated seamen of the
times. Here the sail plan is limited to two square sails
on the fore mast and main mast, with a lateen on the
mizen. A small spritsail is hoisted below the bowsprit.

The Mediterranean peoples appear to have evolved
a compromise vessel, called a " galleas " (Fig. 81), propelled by oars and sails. Three different classes of
pinnaces are pictured in Fig. 82, and were in use by most
of the European powers. Two English ships are shown
in Figs. 83 and 84. The first is similar to the vessels
which withstood the attacks of the Spanish Armada.
The four-master, Fig. 84, shows open stern and quarter
galleries, a greater number of guns at different levels,
and also shows a lateen topsail on the mizen mast. Some
idea of the interior of Elizabethan ships can be gleaned
from Figs. 85 to 88. The former shows the riding bitts on
the gun deck to which the anchor cables were attached
when the ship was at anchor. The whipstaff (Fig. 86) was
a device used to manipulate the tiller for steering purposes. The capstans (Figs. 87, 88) were probably introduced extensively in Elizabethan times and employed to
weigh the anchors, and for other purposes.

X

THE EMPIRE BUILDERS

The period from the middle of the 16th century and onwards has seen a great use of ships for territorial acquisition. European nations vied with each other in overseas discovery, in the acquisition of vast and rich territories, and laid the foundations for the prosperity of succeeding ages.

Ships of the period were in general of considerable similarity. For instance, the Spanish galleon was in substance very like a Flemish or English galleon, although the studious historian will find many differences of detail. The tendency was, however, undoubtedly to a measure of uniformity.

Notable inventions of an earlier age were more extensively incorporated in sailing vessels about this period. The rigging, the number and disposition of the sails, were all improved. The course or main sail was reduced somewhat in size, topsails were increased in height and became more square, and the top-gallant sail somewhat larger and wider. This conduced to greater ease in handling, and provided sails that would stand better and take greater advantage of the wind.

The general aspect of the ships, apart from their sail plan, did not vary greatly from that of the previous age, but marked a steady and natural development. In general, the hulls became larger and higher, and acquired a wealth of ornamentation that can only be described as lavish. The stern and quarter were richly carved (Fig. 90), while the sides of the hull were embellished with carvings

FIG. 89. HUDSON'S *HALF MOON* IN THE ICE.

Circa 1609.

The quest for the north-west passage through the icefloes and gloom of the northern seas.

FIG. 90. STERN VIEW OF A FRENCH WARSHIP.

Circa 1638.

Showing the ornate and elaborate decoration on ships of this period.

FIG. 91. A DUTCH EAST INDIAMAN UNDER CONSTRUCTION.
Circa 1640.

Enormous numbers of oak trees were demolished to supply the timber for one of these great ships.

FIG. 92. A DUTCH WARSHIP.

Circa 1640.

Note how the sail plan is steadily developing.

FIG. 93. ENGLISH LINE-OF-BATTLE SHIP.

Circa 1640.

Here the tiers of guns are features showing the growth of armament.

69

and ornamental work. Gun ports had a tendency to become more regular in arrangement, as the decks were better disposed for the purpose. The hull of an East Indiaman during course of construction is shown in Fig. 91, which will give an idea of the vessels of that time.

Two typical craft of the period 1640 are illustrated in Figs. 92 and 93. In both a similarity exists. In the former, topsails are carried, while in the latter topgallants and royals were hoisted under favourable conditions. The combination of the square and triangular sail on the mizen mast should also be noted. The hulls were lofty and many-decked, often having lengths of 135 to 140 feet, with a breadth of about 46 feet.

During the 17th century the first-rate line-of-battle ships were about 130 feet or more in length, and carried over 100 guns; the second-rates were about 120 feet or longer, and carried eighty to ninety guns; third-rates were about 115 feet in length; and the fourth-rates about 88 feet in length.

A characteristic vessel of the period is illustrated in Fig. 102, which gives a slight idea of the elaborate nature of the stern and quarter cabins and galleries. A famous exploration ship, the *Half Moon*, is pictured in Fig. 89. A Portuguese fisherman, known as a muletta, is shown in Fig. 96, and exhibits a mixture of types and the use of an extraordinary sail plan, including a lateen, triangular or staysail, square sail on a forward projecting mast, and a spritsail beneath the bowsprit.

A gaily decorated Venetian trabaccoto is shown in Fig. 97. It has a mast arrangement reminiscent of the Roman period, the sail gaily decorated in bright colours. These vessels were in use until recently, but were probably of much the same form during the 17th century.

The opening up of the Far East and of the Pacific saw a curious mixture of ship-types. One pictured in Fig. 94, and dated about 1595, has a hull exhibiting

FIG. 94.   A CUBAN SHIP.

Circa 1595.

With a mixture of European, Chinese, and native practice in shipcraft.

FIG. 95.   A JAPANESE JUNK.

Circa 1650.

Making for the shore at the close of day.

FIG. 96. A PORTUGUESE MULETTA.

Circa 1650.

A many-sailed fisherman of peculiar appearance.

FIG. 97. A GAILY DECORATED ITALIAN FISHERMAN.

Circa 1650.

Sails and hull brilliantly coloured as a butterfly.

FIG. 98. A GENOESE GALLEY.

Circa 1650.

The lateen and rowers persisted in Mediterranean waters.

FIG. 99. A FIFTEENTH-CENTURY FISHING BOAT.

Circa 1650.

The forerunner of the present-day luggers.

FIG. 100.　EARLY SOUTHERN CHINESE JUNK.

Circa 1650.

Despite their unwieldy appearance these ships made lengthy voyages.

FIG. 101.　A MERRIMAC " GUNDALOW."

Circa 1700.

A river barge with a form of counterbalanced lateen sail.

74

FIG. 102. AN ENGLISH BATTLESHIP. *Circa* 1680.

Although so comely in appearance these ships were indomitable fighters.

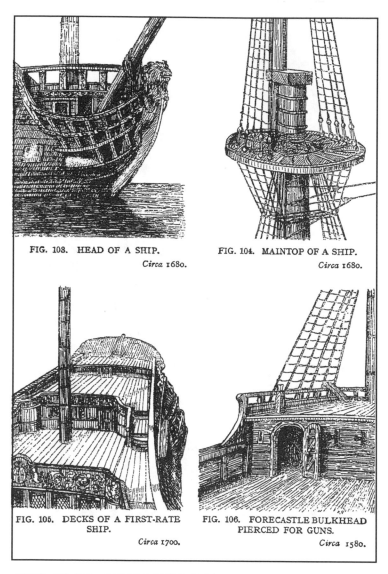

FIG. 103.   HEAD OF A SHIP.

Circa 1680.

FIG. 104.   MAINTOP OF A SHIP.

Circa 1680.

FIG. 105.   DECKS OF A FIRST-RATE
SHIP.

Circa 1700.

FIG. 106.   FORECASTLE BULKHEAD
PIERCED FOR GUNS.

Circa 1580.

FIGS. 103–106.   SOME DETAILS OF EARLY SAILING SHIPS.

SHIP DETAILS

English and Dutch influence. The fore and main sail, composed of bamboos and ratan or matting, are typical of Chinese and Japanese waters. The lateen mizen suggests European influence.

A small early Japanese junk is shown in Fig. 95. It exhibits a small square sail made of matting, while the hull is reminiscent of early Egyptian practice. A Genoese galley hoisting three lateen sails and assisted by rowers is shown in Fig. 98, and indicates the trend of development in Mediterranean waters. Of the small craft the fishermen and coasters were generally of the undecked type, hoisting two lug sails. An early fishing boat is illustrated in Fig. 99.

A peculiar river barge, known as a Merrimac gundalow, is shown in Fig. 101, and an early Southern Chinese junk in Fig. 100.

Some details of hulls and rigging are given in Figs. 103 to 106.

The head of a ship (Fig. 103) shows constructive details; the maintop (Fig. 104) illustrates the main and topmast shrouds.

The elaborate work on the deck erections at the poop of a first-rate ship is shown in Fig. 105, while in Fig. 106 are seen the loopholes and small cannon in the forecastle. The guns were employed to assist in clearing the decks of an invading force.

XI

THE ZENITH OF THE SAILING SHIP

Although the clippers were finer craft than the characteristic ships of the 18th century, they had to withstand the competition due to the introduction of steamships, and for this reason the period 1700 to 1800 probably represents the golden age of the sailing ship. Moreover, some of the finest line-of-battle ships were evolved, while great trading concerns were perfecting a practical sailing vessel able to maintain regular services and communication, and also withstand the attacks of privateers and pirates.

Many different types of ship were in use, ranging from the towering-walled line-of-battle ship to quite small coastal craft. Each was designed for recognised work. For example, the frigate, a fast-sailing armed vessel playing the part of the modern cruiser. They were notable for the disposition of the principal armament on one upper deck. Their lines were finer, and in general they were very good sea-boats. A hull of such a vessel during course of construction is shown in Fig. 112.

Many and strange type names for ships were in use, some being illustrated. A " pink " (Fig. 114) is here shown in the form of a Danish West Indiaman; a Danish " corvette " in Fig. 108, and a " snow " in Fig. 115. The latter was notable for a spar parallel to the main mast, upon which the gaff of the trysail was hoisted. The " hoy," a single-master, is shown in Fig. 107, and a Revenue cutter in Fig. 116, both somewhat similarly rigged. The latter carried a considerable armament of small guns. A three-masted French lugger, " Chasse-

FIG. 107.　A " HOY."

Circa 1730.

A handy ship, extensively used about 1700–1750.

FIG. 108.　A DANISH CORVETTE.

Circa 1750.

The quarter gallery and head are reminiscent of earlier days.

FIG. 109.   A BRITISH EAST INDIAMAN.

Circa 1750.

Ships of the B.E.I. Co. were amongst the finest of their type.

FIG. 110.   A FRENCH LUGGER OR " CHASSE-MARÉE."

Circa 1775.

A typical French fishing boat.

FIG. 111. A DUTCH " BOIER."

Circa 1780.

A ship as typical of Holland as the Dutch windmill.

FIG. 112. A FRIGATE UNDER CONSTRUCTION ON THE
LAUNCHING WAYS.

Circa 1780.

The hull is of shapely and pleasing form.

FIG. 113. A SPANISH XEBEC.

Circa 1783.

The persistence of the Latin tradition is seen in the Xebec, used at the attack on Algiers.

FIG. 114. A DANISH " PINK " USED IN THE WEST INDIAN
SERVICE.

Circa 1790.

Distinguished from the frigate by the absence of a mizen top-gallant sail.

FIG. 115.   A " SNOW."

Circa 1790

Somewhat like a brig, but having a square mizen and trysail set on a separate mast.

FIG. 116.   A BRITISH REVENUE CUTTER.

Circa 1800.

Used to suppress the smuggling so prevalent about this period.

FIG. 117.　A COLLIER OR " GEORDIE " BRIG.

Circa 1780.

Ships of this type carried the bulk of London's coal.

FIG. 118. SCHOONER-RIGGED SLOOP-OF-WAR.

Circa 1780.

Small fast sailing ships employed on naval service.

FIG. 119. THE STERN OF A SECOND-RATE 98-GUN LINE-OF-
BATTLE SHIP.

Circa 1800.

Showing the galleries and decorative work.

FIG. 120. THE BOWS OF A FIRST-RATE 100-GUN WARSHIP.

Circa 1800.

Ships of this class fought at Trafalgar.

FIG. 121. AN AMERICAN SCHOONER OR BLOCK ISLAND BOAT.

Circa 1820.

For coastal and fishery purposes.

FIG. 122. AN AMERICAN WHALER.

Circa 1850.

Built at New Bedford, Mass., U.S.A. This shows some differences from European practice.

FIG. 123. A BARBARY FELUCCA.

Circa 1860.

Piratical craft, often causing innocent seamen considerable alarm.

FIG. 124. RED SEA OR MUSCAT DHOWS.

Circa 1860.

Arab ships capable of lengthy voyages.

marée" (Fig. 110), is still in use in approximately the same form.

In the Mediterranean the traditional galley form was still in use, and Fig. 113 shows a Spanish xebec. A typical East Indiaman is illustrated in Fig. 109, a characteristic Dutch "boier" in Fig. 116, while an American whaler is illustrated in Fig. 122. The coal trade was largely handled by the collier or "Geordie" brigs (Fig. 117), of which large numbers were in use. The sloop-of-war (Fig. 118) was a light, armed vessel extensively used in most parts of the world. A line-of-battle ship mounting 100 to 120 guns was an impressive sight. The stern of a second-rate of ninety-eight guns of about 1800 is shown in Fig. 119, and the bows of a first-rate craft in Fig. 120, which will give some idea of their appearance.

An American ship known as a Block Island boat, *circa* 1820, is shown in Fig. 121, a Barbary felucca in Fig. 123, and a Red Sea or Muscat dhow in Fig. 124.

XII

THE CLIPPER SHIP

Credit for the evolution of the clipper ship is generally given to the Americans, although the clipper did not reach its zenith until about 1850. The characteristic of the clipper was its vastly improved hull form and the multiplicity of its sails. An essential difference was in the shape of the midship section, and also the proportions of length to beam and draft.

Roughly speaking, the sail plan was rectangular, in contradistinction to the triangular sail plan of earlier vessels. The bows were no longer blunt and rounded, but had a finely modelled and tapering form, retaining a small figurehead, giving place later on to a simple piece of decoration. The run aft, or shape of the stern, is likewise finer, and the hull as a whole exhibits scientific ability and thought in the evolution of a vessel that could be driven easily through the water with a minimum of discomfort to those on board.

Speed of sailing was of paramount importance, as competition in the markets of the world was very keen, especially in the China trade and trade with the Colonies. The widespread peace, coupled with the efficiency of the British Navy in policing the seas, made it possible for merchantmen and passenger vessels to go unarmed, and to devote the whole of the ship to peaceful purposes.

Clipper ships are also notable for the great number of emigrants which they carried round about the period of the great gold rush of 1850-1855. Conditions on board were, however, not in any sense agreeably comparable with modern ideas of ocean passenger traffic. Little or

FIG. 125.   AN EARLY CHINA TEA CLIPPER.

Circa 1850.

Showing studding sails set at the side of the fore and main topsails and topgallant sails.

FIG. 126.   A CLIPPER SHIP.

Circa 1860.

Many emigrants sailed to seek their fortunes in ships of this type.

FIG. 127.   A BLACKWALL FRIGATE.

Circa 1875.

A full-rigged ship, iron built, at Blackwall, London, from whence many famous clippers were launched.

FIG. 128.   A COLONIAL CLIPPER.

Circa 1880.

Showing fore and aft sails set on stays between the masts.

FIG. 129.   A FOUR-MASTED STEEL BARQUE.

Circa 1892.

Graceful ships, the most beautiful product of the shipwright's art.

FIG. 130. A BARQUE-RIGGED COLONIAL CLIPPER.

Circa 1866.

The Colonies were dependent on this class of ship for communication with the Motherland.

no accommodation was provided for the emigrants, who had to cook their own meals and generally provide their own food. For beauty of appearance, no other class of vessel can compare with the clipper. They are veritable queens of the ocean. The speed of clippers often attained 18 knots, beating the average modern tramp steamer, and exceeded only by the fastest and best of modern liners.

Early clippers were timber-built, and many of them rigged as barques. Later vessels had iron or steel hulls, steel masts, and carried auxiliary machinery for handling the sails. The early clippers hoisted four comparatively large square sails on a mast, but these were speedily abandoned for a greater number of smaller sails which were easier to handle, while in the craze for speed and record voyages all manner of additional sails were piled on.

The sail above the top-gallant was known as the royal. Above this was sometimes hoisted another, known as a skysail, while a few captains, under favourable conditions, hoisted still another, known as a moon-raker. Another device extensively employed during the clipper period, although it had been known in the 14th century or earlier, was the use of additional sails at the side of the principal ones, known as studding sails, shown in Fig. 125. Extensive use was made of fore-and-aft sails, which are clearly shown in Figs. 128 and 129. These were hoisted on stays between the masts.

Some of the most famous clippers were built on the Thames at Blackwall. A frigate of about the period 1860 is pictured in Fig. 126, and a later frigate in Fig. 127, while a colonial clipper barque is shown in Fig. 130. At this time a quaint fancy was to paint the hulls in bands of black and white, and paint dummy ports in black upon them, a picturesque treatment that accorded well with the beauty of the sail plan. This in later times, however, gave place to the more serviceable, but drab, black or grey.

XIII

MODERN SHIP-TYPES

Despite the vast changes that have taken place over a long period extending into the dim recesses of the past, there are yet to be found on the waters of the world examples of almost all known types of sailing vessel either on active service or still existing for such humble purposes as store ships, coal hulks, and the like. It is impossible in the available space to include every class of sailing ship, but a number are illustrated.

Traditional and geographical considerations have to a large extent determined the persistence of ship-types in any given water. More especially is this noticed in the case of small coasting craft. For instance, the Dutch ship (Fig. 131) retaining the lee board shown raised on the side of the hull is peculiarly adapted to the shallow waters of Holland. Contrast this with the naval sailing pinnace (Fig. 132), a ship's boat carried on board men-of-war and used for harbour services and other duties.

Another form is shown in Fig. 133, which is a single-master, and a typical pleasure cutter hoisting gaff and boom mainsail, top sail, jib, and fore sail. A very handy small sailing vessel with a yawl rig forms the subject of Fig. 135. The yawl is distinguished by the mizen mast mounted on the counter or overhanging part of the stern, whereas in the ketch the mizen mast is before the stern post.

A typical West of England fishing boat, the Penzance lugger (Fig. 134), is characterised by a large lug mounted on the mizen and extended by a sheet reeving through

FIG. 131.　A DUTCH SCHUYT.

The lee board is retained and lifted when passing shallow water.

FIG. 132.　A NAVAL PINNACE.

Carried aboard a man-of-war for harbour and other services.

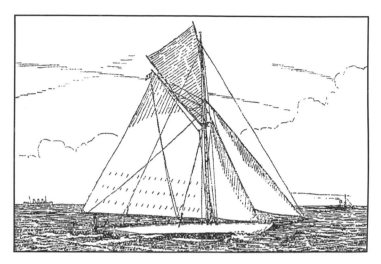

FIG. 133. A RACING CUTTER YACHT.

Built for love of the sea and sport.

FIG. 134. A PENZANCE LUGGER.

Picturesque and sturdy boats that brave the wild Atlantic.

a block at the end of a long pole, or "boomkin," project-ing from the stern. Another picturesque and well-known type is the Thames barge (Fig. 136). Here the main sail is spread by means of a sprit, a long boom reaching from the upper corner of the sail and hoisted on the main mast.

The schooner class embraces a great many different vessels. This rig, as adapted to racing or pleasure yachts, is shown in Fig. 137. It is a complete fore-and-aft rig,

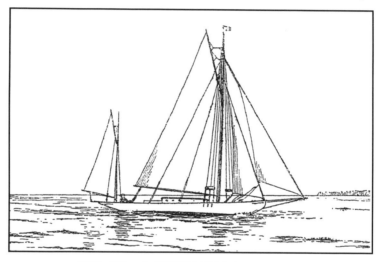

FIG. 135. A YAWL-RIGGED YACHT.

A very handy rig for small ships.

is easy to handle, and has been developed in quite large commercial coasters. An American schooner (Fig. 138) shows a pilot boat such as may have been seen in the waters of Chesapeake Bay. The topmast staysail hoisted between the masts is a characteristic and interesting feature.

A very popular coaster is the topsail schooner (Fig. 139). Here two or more square sails are set on the foremast, making a handy rig for coasting craft. A some-

FIG. 136. A THAMES BARGE.

Familiar to all dwellers along the lower reaches of the Thames.

what similar rig, but without the gaff fore sail, is known as the brigantine; the fore mast in this case sets only square sails, the main mast a main sail and topsail, but staysails are used in addition. The barquentine (Fig. 140) is still largely used in the timber and other trades. The fore mast sets square sails, and the main and mizen are rigged similarly to a schooner. They are easy to handle and economical of labour.

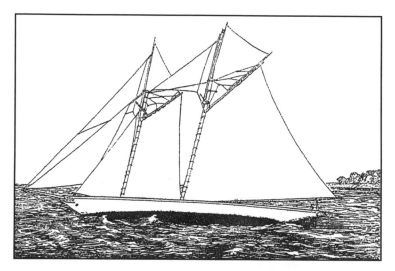

FIG. 137. A RACING SCHOONER.

The four-masted barquentine shown in Fig. 141 is often used in the American timber trade. In the example illustrated the timber port in the bows is shown, this being provided to enable the long baulks of timber to be introduced and unloaded from the vessel, as without such provision the task would be very difficult, if not impossible. In the American trade—especially the routes across the trade winds—multi-masted schooners are utilised. Fig. 142 shows a five-masted schooner, and Fig. 143 a seven-masted steel schooner. These vessels

FIG. 138.   A CHESAPEAKE BAY PILOT BOAT.

The sail plan is a notable feature.

FIG. 139.   A TOPSAIL SCHOONER.

A picturesque survivor of bygone days.

FIG. 140. A BARQUENTINE.

Employed in the timber trade and for coastal and European trade.

FIG. 141. A FOUR-MASTED BARQUENTINE.

Showing timber port in the bows.

FIG. 142. FIVE-MASTED SCHOONER.

Efficient and economical, but lacking the beauty of earlier ships.

FIG. 143. A SEVEN-MASTED STEEL SCHOONER.

A modern product of commercial efficiency.

FIG. 144.   SAFE AT LAST!   THE RETURN OF THE LIFEBOAT.

"A friend in need, a friend indeed."

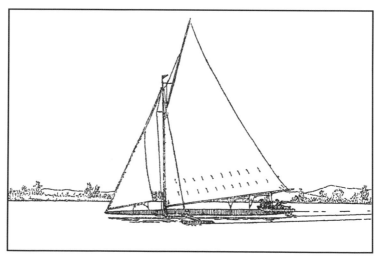

FIG. 145.   AN ICE YACHT AT SPEED.

Ice-yachting is one of the most exhilarating sports.

can hardly be compared for beauty with ships of the clipper class; indeed, they have been designed solely from the commercial standpoint. With their steel hulls and masts, regular sail plan, aided by auxiliary machinery for handling the sails, and other apparatus, they are extremely economical, require a small crew, and can carry a large cargo.

No story of the sailing ship can even be approximately complete without some reference to the sailing lifeboat, a craft that first appeared in 1789, and has been evolved only within comparatively modern times. Its duties consist solely in the saving of life at sea (Fig. 144). There are many variations in the rig of sailing lifeboats, but in general two lug sails are used. Although steam and the petrol engine are displacing the sailing lifeboat, these small craft still continue to add to their laurels by yearly increasing the number of lives snatched from a watery grave.

One type of lifeboat is self-righting, provided with buoyancy tanks to prevent it sinking, and generally designed in such a way as to be able to live through the most severe weather. In many respects it is not unlike the earlier Norse ship. Perhaps the lifeboat is the only truly universal craft. It knows neither nations nor creeds, it saves life of either friend or foe with equal disregard. No weather is too heavy for the lifeboat to put to sea, and it is seldom it returns without having added further laurels to the proud record held by the Royal National Lifeboat Institution, a voluntarily supported organisation which maintains these vessels in their remarkable state of efficiency.

A sailing boat used on ice is shown in Fig. 145, examples being found where suitable ice is prevalent, as in Holland and America.

XIV

AUXILIARY VESSELS

Only brief mention can be made of the hybrid class of sailing ship, although many examples are worth mentioning. Known as a class as "auxiliaries," they are characterised by the use of sails for propulsion under normal conditions, aided by steam or oil engines. Both large and small craft are utilised in this way. Coaster and fishing vessels are yearly being equipped as auxiliaries.

Sea-going early steamers had engines which either were frankly auxiliary or were little better. They were full rigged. This was because engines were not then trustworthy, and because they were extravagant in coal, of which enough could not, therefore, be carried for a long passage. Even in the Russian War of 1854-1855 British steam men-of-war were really only auxiliary. This period dates from the late thirties, and it was not until *circa* 1880-1890 that sails were abolished both in ocean steamers and men-of-war.

For exploration work, mission purposes, and other duties, auxiliary craft are found in many parts of the world. Fig. 146 shows the *Nimrod*, originally a Dundee whaler, to which steam machinery was added, the whole making an admirable combination for exploration in polar regions. The mission ship, Fig. 147, relies primarily upon its sails for propulsion, but has resource to oil engines during calm weather.

FIG. 146. AN EXPLORATION SHIP. THE *NIMROD*.

Sir Ernest Shackleton and other explorers have used ships of this general type.

FIG. 147. AN AUXILIARY SCHOONER.

On missionary work, carrying the comfort of the Church to mariners on lonely seas.

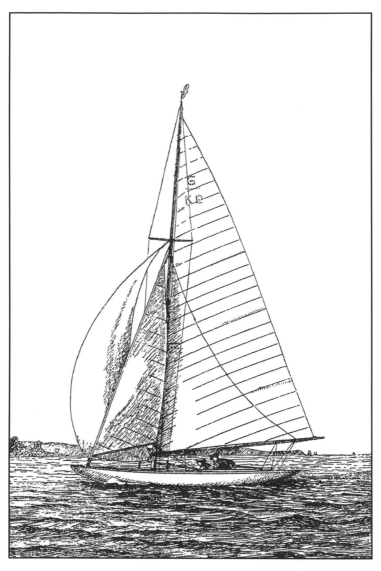

FIG. 148.   A SIX-METRE YACHT, BERMUDA RIGGED.

A class extensively adopted for international yacht races.

XV

CONTEMPORARY VESSELS

Volumes could be devoted to contemporary vessels but only a few can be dealt with here. Perhaps one of the greatest features of contemporary vessels is the lavish care bestowed upon their scientific design. This finds its greatest achievement in the modern racing yacht. Built to pre-determined formulæ and to some specific rating or class, many diverse forms of vessel have been produced by the most able designers.

The modern yacht is, however, a scientific creation, founded on technical knowledge, fashioned with the skill and loving care of the artist and craftsman. As examples, two diverse types are illustrated. Fig. 148 shows a 6-metre racing yacht such as used in international competitions, and Fig. 149 a light Thames canoe, a craft that provides wonderful sport on the upper reaches of the Thames.

The novelty of sailing ships is reserved till the last, and time alone can decide whether it is as good, better, or worse than any previous sailing vessel. The Rotor ship (Fig. 150) is classed as a sailing vessel, as it uses the power of the wind for its propulsion. It has, however, no sails in the practical sense, their place being taken by two lofty metal cylinders. These are suitably mounted and so arranged that they can be rotated by means of auxiliary machinery. These cylinders are about 60 feet in height and 10 feet in diameter, and are rotated at about 100 revolutions per minute, on a ship about 150 feet in length. The principle is based on the effect noted by

FIG. 149. THAMES CANOES.

Light and sporty little boats with a remarkable turn of speed.

FIG. 150. A SAILING SHIP WITH MECHANICAL SAILS.

Revolving cylinders take the place of sails.

MECHANICAL SAILS

Magnus in 1853, and it is claimed that by suitably rotating the cylinders the ship can drive forward, although the wind may be blowing on the beam or side of the vessel. On trial a speed of about 8 knots has been attained.

It is claimed that greater manœuvring power and ability to sail close against the wind is obtained with this craft, and that a more effective driving power is derived from the cylinders than from an equal area of sail.

WORKS OF REFERENCE

In the preparation of this little book the author has studied many works of reference, some of which are mentioned below. To all of them he desires to acknowledge his indebtedness, and to suggest that the student should peruse them and all other sources of information.

Much useful knowledge is to be found in the public and other museums and libraries where models and old prints are available, as well as in the pages of contemporary periodicals dealing with nautical subjects.

A SHORT BIBLIOGRAPHY

ANCIENT AND MODERN SHIPS. Sir George Holmes.
ANCIENT SHIPS. Cecil Torr.
BLACKWALL FRIGATES. E. Lubbock.
BRITISH MERCANTILE MARINE. E. Blackmoor.
COLONIAL CLIPPERS. E. Lubbock.
DICTIONARY OF SEA TERMS. A. Ansted.
ENCYCLOPÆDIA BRITANNICA.
SEAMANSHIP. Sir George Nares.
SHIPBUILDER'S ASSISTANT. W. Sutherland.
SAILING SHIP MODELS. R. Morton Nance.
SHIPS AND WAYS OF OTHER DAYS. E. Keble Chatterton.
HISTORY OF MARINE ARCHITECTURE. C. Charnock.
THE ROYAL NAVY. W. Laird Clowes.
OLD SHIP FIGURE HEADS AND STERNS. L. G. Carr Laughton.
THE SHIP, HER STORY. W. Clarke Russell.
MANUAL OF YACHT AND BOAT SAILING AND ARCHITEC-
 TURE. Dixon Kemp.
TRUCK TO KEEL. P. Paasch.

PERIODICALS.

" THE MARINERS' MIRROR." "THE RUDDER."
" THE YACHTING MONTHLY." "THE SHIPBUILDER."
" NAVY AND ARMY."

PUBLIC EXHIBITIONS AND MUSEUMS

SCIENCE MUSEUM. South Kensington, London.
MUSÉE DE MARINE. The Louvre, Paris.
ROYAL NAVAL MUSEUM. Greenwich.
UNITED SERVICES MUSEUM. Whitehall, London.

Publications by Algrove Publishing Limited

The following is a list of titles from our popular "*Classic Reprint Series*" as well as a list of other publications by *Algrove Publishing Limited.*

Classic Reprint Series

Item #	Title
49L8024	☐ 1800 MECHANICAL MOVEMENTS AND DEVICES
49L8055	☐ 970 MECHANICAL APPLIANCES AND NOVELTIES OF CONSTRUCTION
49L8038	☐ A BOOK OF ALPHABETS WITH PLAIN, ORNAMENTAL, ANCIENT AND MEDIAEVAL STYLES
49L8074	☐ ARE YOU A GENIUS? WHAT IS YOUR I.Q?
49L8101	☐ ARTS-CRAFTS LAMPS & SHADES — *HOW TO MAKE THEM*
49L8016	☐ BARN PLANS & OUTBUILDINGS
49L8046	☐ BEAUTIFYING THE HOME GROUNDS
49L8090	☐ BOAT-BUILDING AND BOATING
49L8014	☐ BOOK OF TRADES
49L8004	☐ BOULTON & PAUL, LTD. 1898 CATALOGUE
49L8012	☐ BOY CRAFT
49L8077	☐ CAMP COOKERY
49L8082	☐ CANADIAN WILD FLOWERS
49L8072	☐ CLASSIC PUZZLES AND HOW TO SOLVE THEM
49L8048	☐ CLAY MODELLING AND PLASTER CASTING
49L8005	☐ COLONIAL FURNITURE
49L8065	☐ COPING SAW WORK
49L8032	☐ DECORATIVE CARVING, PYROGRAPHY AND FLEMISH CARVING
49L8092	☐ DETAIL, COTTAGE AND CONSTRUCTIVE ARCHITECTURE
49L8086	☐ FARM BLACKSMITHING
49L8031	☐ FARM MECHANICS
49L8029	☐ FARM WEEDS OF CANADA
49L8015	☐ FENCES, GATES & BRIDGES
49L8056	☐ FLORA'S LEXICON
49L8087	☐ FORGING
49L8706	☐ FROM LOG TO LOG HOUSE
49L8091	☐ FURNITURE DESIGNING AND DRAUGHTING
49L8049	☐ HANDBOOK OF TURNING
49L8027	☐ HANDY FARM DEVICES AND HOW TO MAKE THEM
49L0720	☐ HOMES & INTERIORS OF THE 1920'S
49L8002	☐ HOW TO PAINT SIGNS & SHO' CARDS
49L8054	☐ HOW TO USE THE STEEL SQUARE
49L8001	☐ LEE'S PRICELESS RECIPES
49L8078	☐ MANUAL OF SEAMANSHIP FOR BOYS AND SEAMEN OF THE ROYAL NAVY, 1904
49L8020	☐ MISSION FURNITURE, HOW TO MAKE IT
49L8081	☐ MR. PUNCH WITH ROD AND GUN — *THE HUMOUR OF FISHING AND SHOOTING*
49L8073	☐ NAME IT! THE PICTORIAL QUIZ BOOK
49L8033	☐ ORNAMENTAL AND DECORATIVE WOOD CARVINGS
49L8089	☐ OVERSHOT WATER WHEELS FOR SMALL STREAMS
49L8059	☐ PROJECTS FOR WOODWORK TRAINING
49L8705	☐ REFLECTIONS ON THE FUNGALOIDS
49L8003	☐ RUSTIC CARPENTRY
49L8044	☐ SAM LOYD'S PICTURE PUZZLES
49L8030	☐ SHELTERS, SHACKS & SHANTIES
49L8085	☐ SKELETON LEAVES AND PHANTOM FLOWERS
49L8068	☐ SPECIALIZED JOINERY
49L8052	☐ STANLEY COMBINATION PLANES — *THE 45, THE 50 & THE 55*
49L8050	☐ STRONG'S BOOK OF DESIGNS
49L8064	☐ THE ARCHITECTURE OF COUNTRY HOUSES
49L8034	☐ THE ART OF WHITTLING
49L8018	☐ THE BOY'S BOOK OF MECHANICAL MODELS
49L8071	☐ THE BULL OF THE WOODS, VOL.1
49L8080	☐ THE BULL OF THE WOODS, VOL.2
45L0106	☐ THE DUCHESS OF BLOOMSBURY STREET
49L8021	☐ THE INTERNATIONAL CYCLOPEDIA OF MONOGRAMS
49L8053	☐ THE METALWORKING LATHE
49L8023	☐ THE OPEN TIMBER ROOFS OF THE MIDDLE AGES
49L8076	☐ THE WILDFLOWERS OF AMERICA
49L8057	☐ THE WILDFLOWERS OF CANADA
49L8058	☐ THE YANKEE WHALER
49L8025	☐ THE YOUNG SEA OFFICER'S SHEET ANCHOR
49L8047	☐ TIMBER — *FROM THE FOREST, TO ITS USE IN COMMERCE*
49L8061	☐ TRADITIONS OF THE NAVY
49L8042	☐ TURNING FOR AMATEURS
49L8039	☐ VIOLIN MAKING AS IT WAS, AND IS
49L8079	☐ WILLIAM BULLOCK & CO. — *HARDWARE CATALOG, CIRCA 1850*
49L8019	☐ WINDMILLS AND WIND MOTORS
49L8013	☐ YOU CAN MAKE IT
49L8035	☐ YOU CAN MAKE IT FOR CAMP & COTTAGE
49L8036	☐ YOU CAN MAKE IT FOR PROFIT

Other Algrove Publications

Item #	Title
49L8601	☐ ALL THE KNOTS YOU NEED (HARD COVER)
49L8602	☐ ALL THE KNOTS YOU NEED (SOFT COVER)
49L8707	☐ BUILDING THE NORWEGIAN SAILING PRAM (MANUAL AND PLANS)
49L8708	☐ BUILDING THE SEA URCHIN (MANUAL AND PLANS)
49L8084	☐ THE ART OF ARTHUR WATTS
49L8067	☐ WOOD HANDBOOK — *WOOD AS AN ENGINEERING MATERIAL*
49L8060	☐ WOODEN PLANES AND HOW TO MAKE THEM